NEWwoman

BlokeJokes 2

Text copyright © Hatchette Emap Magazines Limited, 2001
Design and artwork copyright © Carlton Books Limited, 2001

This edition published 2002 For Index Books Ltd

A CIP catalogue record for this book is available from the British Library.

ISBN 1 84222 373 9

Editorial Manager: Venetia Penfold
Senior Art Editor: Barbara Zuñiga
Editor: Louise Johnson
Production: Garry Lewis
Illustrations: Sarah Nayler

www.newwoman.co.uk

NEWwoman

Edited by **Louise Johnson**

BlokeJokes 2

... because men
are still funny

CONTENTS

1

GREAT MYSTERIES OF OUR TIME (1) ... WHY?

Why do **blokes** get **married**?

So they don't have to hold their stomachs in anymore.

Why did the **bloke** put **Viagra** in his eyes?
He wanted to look hard.

Why do women need blokes?
Because vibrators can't get a round of drinks in.

Why do **blokes** like **smart women**?
Opposites attract.

Why do blokes keep empty milk bottles in the fridge?
In case anyone wants their coffee black.

Why do **blokes** have **legs**?
So their brains don't drag on the floor.

Why do blokes whistle when they're
sitting on the toilet?
So they can remember which end to wipe.

Why is **Santa** such a **happy bloke**?

Because he knows where all the bad girls live.

Why do blokes want to marry virgins?

Because they can't stand criticism.

Why can't **blokes** make **ice cubes**?

They don't know the recipe.

Why do blokes propose?

Because they can't afford our wages!

Why do **little boys** whine?

Because they're practising to be blokes.

Why was Colonel Sanders a typical bloke?

All he cared about were legs, breasts and thighs.

Why do **blokes** need **instant replay** on **TV sports**?

Because after 30 seconds they forget what happened.

Why are bankers good lovers?

They know the penalty for early withdrawals.

Why did the **bloke** cross the **road**?

God knows, why do they bother doing anything?

Why did the **bloke** ask all his **friends** to **save** their **burnt-out** light bulbs?

Because he was trying to build a darkroom.

Why does a **penis** have a **hole** in the **end**?

So blokes can be open-minded.

Why does it snow at Christmas?

Because Santa's coming.

Why shouldn't you hit a bloke with glasses?

A baseball bat is much more effective.

Why did the **stupid bloke** get a **stabbing pain** in his **eye** every time he drank a **cup of tea**?

He forgot to take the spoon out.

Why should you **never** try to find a bloke's **inner child**?

Because you'll have enough trouble coping with his outer one.

Why were blokes given larger brains than dogs?

So they wouldn't hump women's legs at cocktail parties.

Why don't **single** women **fart**?

Because they don't get a bum till they're married.

Why are **women** more **intelligent** than blokes?

Because diamonds are a girl's best friend ... while man's best friend is a dog.

Why does it take **one million** sperm to **fertilise** just **one egg**?

Because they come from a bloke, so they won't stop to ask for directions.

Why did God put blokes' sexual organs on the outside?

So they remember where they are.

Why don't women have blokes' brains?

Because they don't have penises to keep them in.

Why do men like to make salads?

Because they're born tossers.

2

EVERYONE LIKES A LIST, DON'T THEY?

New Training Courses For Men

- Introduction To Common Household Objects I: The Mop.
- Introduction To Common Household Objects II: The Iron.
- Fridge Forensics: Identifying And Removing The Dead.

- Design Pattern Or Splatter Stain On The Lino?:
  You CAN Tell The Difference!
- Accepting Loss I: If It's Empty, You Can Throw It Away.
- Accepting Loss II: If The Milk Expired Three Weeks Ago,
  Keeping It In The Fridge Won't Bring It Back.
- Recycling Skills I: Boxes That The Electronics Came In.
- Recycling Skills II: Polystyrene That Came In The Boxes
  That The Electronics Came In.
- Bathroom Etiquette I: How To Remove Shaving Stubble
  From The Sink.
- Bathroom Etiquette II: Let's Wash Those Towels!

- Bathroom Etiquette III: Five Easy Ways To Tell When You're About To Run Out Of Toilet Paper!
- Retro? Or Just Hideous?: Re-examining Your '80s Lairy Shirts.
- No, The Dishes Won't Wash Themselves: Knowing The Limitations Of Your Kitchenware.
- Going Out To Dinner: Beyond Pizza Hut.
- Expand Your Entertainment Options: Renting Videos That Don't Fall Into The 'Action/Adventure' Category.
- Yours, Mine And Ours: Sharing The Remote.
- Adventures In Housekeeping I: Let's Clean The Toilet.

- Adventures In Housekeeping II: Let's Clean Under The Bed.
- Listening: It's Not Just Something You Do During Half-Time.
- Accepting Your Limitations: Just Because You Have Power Tools Doesn't Mean You Can Fix It.

Ten Things Blokes Know About Women:

1.
2.
3.
4.
5.
6.
7.
8.
9.
10. They have tits.

More Harsh Things A Woman Can Say To A Naked Bloke . . .

- Ahhhh, it's cute.
- Make it dance.
- Can I paint a smiley face on it?
- It's OK, we'll work around it.
- Will it squeak if I squeeze it?
- Oh no . . . a flash headache.
- (Giggle and point)
- Can I be honest with you?
- How sweet, you brought incense.
- That explains your car.
- At least this won't take long.
- It looks so unused.
- Why don't we skip right to the cigarettes?
- If you get me really drunk first.
- Is that an optical illusion?
- What *is* that?
- It's a good thing you have so many other talents.
- Does it come with an air pump?
- So this is why you're supposed to judge people on personality.

What Women Want In A Bloke

Original List (Age 22)

1. Handsome.
2. Charming.
3. Financially successful.
4. A caring listener.
5. Witty.
6. In good shape.
7. Dresses with style.
8. Appreciates the finer things.
9. Full of thoughtful surprises.
10. An imaginative, romantic lover.

Revised List (Age 32)

1. Nice-looking – preferably with hair on his head.
2. Opens car doors, pulls out chairs.
3. Has enough money for a nice dinner at a restaurant.
4. Listens more than he talks.
5. Laughs at my jokes at appropriate times.
6. Can carry in all groceries with ease.
7. Owns at least one tie.
8. Appreciates a good home-cooked meal.
9. Remembers birthdays and anniversaries.
10. Seeks romance at least once a week.

Revised List (Age 42)

1. Not too ugly – bald head OK.
2. Doesn't drive off until I'm in the car.
3. Works steadily – splurges on dinner at McDonald's on occasion.
4. Nods head at appropriate times when I'm talking.
5. Usually remembers the punchlines of jokes.
6. Is in good enough shape to rearrange furniture.
7. Usually wears shirt that covers stomach.
8. Knows not to buy champagne with screw-top lids.
9. Remembers to put the toilet seat lid down.
10. Shaves on most weekends.

Revised List (Age 52)

1. Keeps hair in nose and ears trimmed to appropriate length.
2. Doesn't belch or scratch in public.
3. Doesn't borrow money too often.
4. Doesn't nod off to sleep while I'm talking.
5. Doesn't re-tell the same jokes too many times.
6. Is in good enough shape to get off couch on weekends.
7. Usually wears matching socks and fresh underwear.
8. Appreciates a good TV dinner.
9. Remembers your name on occasion.
10. Shaves on some weekends.

Revised List (Age 62)

1. Doesn't scare small children.
2. Remembers where bathroom is.
3. Doesn't require much money for upkeep.
4. Only snores lightly when awake (LOUDLY when asleep).
5. Doesn't forget why he's laughing.
6. Is in good enough shape to stand up by himself.
7. Usually wears some clothes.
8. Likes soft foods.
9. Remembers where he left his teeth.
10. Remembers when ...

Revised List (Age 72)

1. Breathing ...

More Cutting Put-Downs For Blokes Who Really Deserve Them

- 'You know you said you wanted to make love to me really badly – well, you've succeeded!'
- '100,000 sperm and you were the fastest?'
- 'You're depriving some poor village of its idiot.'
- 'Save your breath – you'll need it to blow up the only date you'll get tonight.'
- 'If I throw a stick, will you leave?'
- 'A hard-on doesn't count as personal growth.'
- 'I can't be your type – I'm not inflatable.'

Why Are Blokes Like Computers?

- They're hard to figure out and never have enough memory.
- They're supposed to help you solve your problems, but half the time, they are the problem.
- As soon as you commit to one, you realise that if you'd waited a little longer, you could've had a better model.

Why Are Women Brighter Than Blokes?

- We got off the *Titanic* first.
- We can scare bloke bosses with mysterious gynaecological disorder excuses.
- We don't look like a frog in a blender when dancing.
- We don't have to fart to amuse ourselves.
- If we forget to shave, no-one has to know.
- We can congratulate our team-mate without ever touching her rear.
- We have the ability to dress ourselves.
- We never have to reach down every so often to make sure our privates are still there.

- We can talk to people of the opposite sex without having to picture them naked.
- If we marry someone 20 years younger, we're aware that we look like an idiot.
- We know that there are times when chocolate really can solve all your problems.
- We'll never regret piercing our ears.
- We never ejaculate prematurely.
- We can fully assess a person just by looking at their shoes.
- We can make comments about how stupid blokes are in their presence, because they aren't listening anyway.

A Christmas Tree Is Better Than A Bloke Because . . .

A Christmas tree is always erect.

*

Even small ones give satisfaction.

*

A Christmas tree stays up for 12 days and nights.

*

A Christmas tree always looks good – even with the lights on.

*

A Christmas tree is always happy with its size.

*

A Christmas tree has cute balls.

*

A Christmas tree doesn't get mad if you break one of its balls.

*

You can throw a Christmas tree out when it starts looking scruffy.

*

You don't have to put up with a Christmas tree all year.

New Drugs On The Market

Following the success of Viagra, pharmaceutical companies are experimenting with a whole range of drugs designed to improve the performance of blokes in today's society. Here are some of the most promising ...

- **BUYAGRA** – Married and otherwise attached blokes reported a sudden urge to buy their womenfolk expensive jewellery and gifts after taking this drug for just two days. Still to be seen: whether this drug can encourage them to stretch to a new designer wardrobe and an exotic holiday too.

- **COMPLIMENTRA** – In clinical trials, 82% of middle-aged blokes given this drug noticed that their wives had a new hairstyle. Currently being tested to see if its effects can extend to noticing new clothing.

• **FLYAGRA** – This drug is showing special promise in treating blokes with OFD (open-fly disorder). Especially useful for blokes on Viagra.

• **DIRECTRA** – A dose of this drug given to blokes before leaving on car trips caused 72 per cent of them to stop and ask directions when they got lost, compared to a control group of 0.2 per cent.

• **NEGA-SPORTAGRA** – Blokes reported that this drug had the strange effect of making them want to turn off televised sports and actually chat to their girlfriends.

3

IT'S A BIBLE THING!

One day in the Garden of Eden, Eve calls out to God: 'Lord, I have a problem.'

'What's the problem, Eve?'

'Lord, I know you've created me and have provided this beautiful garden and all of these wonderful animals, and that hilarious snake, but I'm just not happy.'

'Why is that, Eve?' came the reply from above.

'Lord, I am lonely, and sick of apples.'

'Well, Eve, in that case I have a solution. I shall create a bloke for you.'

'What's a bloke, Lord?'

'This bloke will be a flawed creature, with aggressive tendencies, an enormous ego, and an inability to empathise or listen to you properly. All in all, he'll give you a hard time. But he'll be bigger and faster, and more muscular than you. He'll be really good at fighting and kicking a ball about and hunting, and not all that bad in the sack.'

'Sounds great,' says Eve, with an ironically raised eyebrow.

'Yeah, well, you can have him on one condition,' says God. 'Because of his tender ego, you'll have to let him think I made him first. Just remember, it's our little secret ... **You know, woman to woman.'**

A bloke says to God: 'God, why did you make woman so beautiful?'
God says: 'So you would love her.'
'But God,' the bloke says. 'Why did you make her so dumb?'
God says: **'So she would love you.'**

One day three blokes were out walking and came upon a raging, violent river. They needed to get to the other side, but didn't know how.

The first bloke prayed to God, saying: 'Please God, give me the strength to cross this river.'

Poof! God gave him big arms and strong legs, and he was able to swim across the river in about two hours.

Seeing this, the second man prayed to God, saying: 'Please God, give me the strength and ability to cross this river.'

Poof! God gave him a rowing boat and he was able to row across the river in about an hour.

The third man saw how this worked out for the other two, so he also prayed to God, saying: 'Please God, give me the strength, ability and courage to cross this river.'

And poof! God turned him into a woman and he walked across the bridge.

When God created man, she was only joking.

What would have happened if it had been **three Wise Women** instead of **three Wise Men**?

They would have asked directions, arrived on time, helped deliver the baby, cleaned the stable, made a casserole and brought practical gifts.

MMM

But what would they have said when they left . . . ?

'Did you see the sandals Mary was wearing with that gown?'

'That baby doesn't look anything like Joseph!'

'Virgin, my arse! I knew her in school!'

'Can you believe they let all of those disgusting animals
in the house?'

'I heard Joseph isn't even working right now!'

'And that donkey they're riding has seen better days, too!'

'Want to bet on how long it'll take to get your casserole dish back?'

Why do only 10 per cent of blokes make it to heaven?

Because if they all went, it would be hell.

Ten Reasons God Created Eve

1. God worried that Adam would always be lost in the Garden because blokes hate to ask for directions.

2. God knew that Adam would one day need someone to hand him the TV remote. (Blokes don't want to see what's ON TV, they want to see WHAT ELSE is on!)

3. God knew that Adam would never buy a new fig leaf when his seat wore out and would need Eve to tell him what an arse he was making of himself.

4. God knew that Adam would never make a doctor's appointment for himself.

5. God knew that Adam would never remember when to put the rubbish out for the dustmen.

6. God knew that if the world was to be populated, blokes would never be able to handle childbearing.

7. As 'Keeper of the Garden', Adam would never remember where he put his tools.

8. The scripture account of creation indicates Adam needed someone to blame his troubles on when God caught him hiding in the Garden.

9. As the Bible says: 'It is not good for man to be alone.'

10. When God finished the creation of Adam, He stepped back, scratched His head and said: 'I can do better than that.'

Why did God create alcohol?

So ugly blokes would get the chance to have sex.

One day The Lord spoke to Adam: 'I've got some good news and some bad news.' Adam looked at The Lord and replied: 'Well, give me the good news first.'

Smiling, The Lord explained: 'I've got two new organs for you. One is called a brain and it will allow you to create new things, solve problems and have intelligent conversations with Eve. The other organ I have for you is called a penis. It will give you great physical pleasure and allow you to reproduce your now-intelligent life form and populate this planet. Eve will be very happy that you now have this organ to give her children.'

Adam, very excited, exclaimed: 'These are great gifts you've given to me. What could possibly be bad news after such great tidings?'

The Lord looked upon Adam and said with great sorrow: 'You'll never be able to use these two gifts at the same time.'

WHAT'S THE DIFFERENCE, ANYWAY?

What's the **difference** between
a **bloke** and a **Brussels sprout**?
One is tasteless and smells of farts
and the other is a nutritious vegetable!

What's the **difference** between a **bloke** and a **vibrator**?
A vibrator won't make you
sleep in the wet patch.

What's the **difference** between **blokes** and **women**?
A woman wants one bloke to satisfy
her every need.
A bloke wants every woman to
satisfy his one need.

What's the **difference** between a **bloke** and **ET**?
ET phones home.

What's the difference between **blokes** and **women**?

Women dream of world peace, a safe environment and eliminating hunger. Blokes dream of being stuck in a lift with Destiny's Child.

What's the **difference** between a single **bloke** and a **married bloke**?

A single bloke will lie awake all night thinking about something you say. A married bloke will fall asleep before you finish.

What's the difference between a bloke and a bird?

A bird can whistle through its pecker.

What's the difference between **blokes' sex talk** and **women's sex talk**?

When a bloke talks dirty to a woman, it's sexual harassment. When a woman talks dirty to a bloke, it's 49p a minute.

What's the difference between women's relationships with their children and blokes'?

Women know about their children's dentist appointments, football games, romances, best friends, favourite foods, secret fears and hopes and dreams. Blokes are vaguely aware of some short people living in the house.

What's the **difference** between a **bloke** and a **catfish**?

One's a bottom-feeding scum-sucker – the other's a fish!

What's the difference between a woman's behaviour during the menopause and a bloke's?

A menopausal woman goes through a variety of complex emotional, psychological and biological changes that vary from individual to individual. The menopause in men provokes an identical reaction – they all buy Raybans sunglasses and leather driving gloves, then go shopping for a Porsche.

5

WHO SAYS BLOKES HAVE ONE-TRACK MINDS?

A bloke walks up to his wife in the kitchen one morning, pinches her on her bottom and says:
'You know, if you firmed this up, we could get rid of your girdle.'

While this was borderline intolerable, she bit her tongue and stayed silent.

The next morning the bloke wakes his wife with a pinch on the boob and says: 'You know, if you firmed these up, we could get rid of your bra.'

This was beyond a joke, so she rolls over and grabs him by the penis. With a death grip in place, she says: 'You know, if you firmed this up, we could get rid of the postman, the gardener, the odd-job man and your brother.'

D ave walks into the bar and sees his mate Jeff huddled over a table, depressed. Dave walks over and asks Jeff what's wrong. 'Well,' replies Jeff. 'You know that beautiful girl at work I wanted to ask out, but couldn't because I got an erection every time I saw her?'

'Yes,' replies Dave with a smile.

'Well,' says Jeff, straightening up. 'I finally plucked up the courage to ask her out, and she agreed.'

'That's great!' says Dave. 'When's the date?'

'I went to meet her this evening,' continues Jeff. 'But because I was worried I'd get an erection again, I got some sticky tape and taped my todger to my leg, so if I did, it wouldn't show.'

'Sensible,' says Dave.

'So I got to her door,' says Jeff, 'and I rang her doorbell. And she answered it in the sheerest, tiniest dress you ever saw.'

'And what happened then?'

Jeff huddles over the table again.

'I kicked her in the face.'

Three women were having a laugh, comparing their blokes' love techniques to cars:

The first says: 'My lover's like a Rolls Royce ... sophisticated and comfortable.'

The second says: 'Mine is like a Ferrari ... fast and powerful.'

The third says: 'Well, my lover's like an old Morris Minor ... you have to start him by hand and jump on when he gets going.'

A bloke is sitting next to a gorgeous woman on a plane. He strikes up a conversation, but then she asks if he minds her reading her book.

Bloke: 'No, not at all! What are you reading?'

Woman: '*The Joy Of Sex*.'

Bloke: 'Hmm. Anything interesting?'

Woman: 'Yeah. Apparently, a man's nationality can indicate things about his penis size.'

Bloke: 'OK, like what?'

Woman: 'Well, Polish men have the longest ones and American Indians have the thickest. Oh, by the way, my name is Laura Smith.'

Bloke: 'Nice to meet you, Laura. My name's Tonto Kawalski.'

A bloke and his wife have separate bedrooms because of his loud snoring. One night when he's feeling amorous, the bloke calls out to his wife. 'Oh, my little boopey-boo, I miss you.'

So his wife gets up and goes to his room, but as she's walking in, she trips on the carpet and falls flat on her face.

'Oh,' he says sweetly. 'Did my little honey-woney hurt her ickle nosey-wosey?'

The woman picks herself up, gets in her husband's bed and they make passionate love.

Afterwards, as she's going back to her room, she once again trips on the carpet and falls flat on her face.

The bloke raises his head from the pillow, looks at his wife lying on the floor and says:

'Clumsy bitch.'

A really good-looking bloke walks into a singles bar, gets a drink and takes a seat. During the course of the evening he tries to chat up every single woman who walks into the bar, with no luck. Suddenly a real pig of a bloke walks in. He sits at the bar, and within seconds he's surrounded by women. Very soon he walks out of the bar with two of the most beautiful women you ever saw. Disheartened by all this, the good-looking bloke goes up to the barman and says: 'Excuse me, but that minging bloke just came in here and left with those two stunning women – what's his secret? He's as ugly as sin and I'm everything a girl could want.' 'Well,' says the barman. 'I don't know how he does it, but the same thing happens every night. He walks in, orders a drink, and just sits there licking his eyebrows … '

A bloke is walking through a hotel lobby when he accidentally bumps into a woman and his elbow digs into her breast. 'Oh, sorry,' he says. 'But if your heart is as soft as your breast, I know you'll forgive me.' And the woman replies: 'And if your penis is as hard as your elbow, I'm in Room 103!!!'

The blind date didn't go well, but as the woman arrives at her door, relieved that the evening is finally over, the bloke suddenly says: 'Do you want to see my underwear?'

Before she can respond, he drops his trousers, right there in the hall, revealing that he isn't wearing any underwear. She glances down and says:

'Nice design – does it also come in men's sizes?'

Two women are having a conversation about their blokes when the first one says: 'My bloke said he fantasised about having two girls at once.'

The other replies: 'Yeah, most blokes do. What did you tell him?'

'I said, "If you can't satisfy one woman, why would you want to piss off two?"'

A young bloke is sitting next to an old priest on a plane, waiting for take-off. There's a minor technical hitch delaying things so the Captain announces that the airline will be serving a round of free drinks. When the lovely air hostess comes by for their order, the bloke asks for a double Scotch. She then asks the priest if he'd like a drink. 'Oh no,' says the priest. 'I'd rather commit adultery than drink alcohol.' Stopping in mid-swallow and dribbling Scotch down his front, the bloke replaces his drink on the hostess's drinks cart. 'Excuse me, miss,' he says. 'I didn't know I had a choice!'

A bloke's sitting in a cinema, and when the usherette asks to see his ticket, he flashes at her. Unfazed, she says:

'I asked to see your ticket
– not your stub!'

A bloke and his girlfriend are just about to have sex when she asks if he's got a condom.
'Of course,' the bloke replies. 'In fact, I bought a special Olympic pack with gold, silver and bronze-coloured ones.' As he starts to put on the gold one, his girlfriend stops him and says: 'Could you put the silver one on?' When the bloke asks why, she replies: 'So you come second for a change!'

Tell this one to a bloke to wind him up ...

Have you heard that women's orgasms can be categorised into one of four types? They are the Positive Orgasm, the Negative Orgasm, the Holy Orgasm and the Fake Orgasm.

It's really easy to identify them, too:

When having a Positive Orgasm, a woman will cry:

'Oh yes, oh yes ... oh yes!'

When having a Negative Orgasm, a woman will cry:

'Oh no, no ... oh no!'

When having a Holy Orgasm, she'll cry:

'Oh God, oh God ... oh, God!'

When having a Fake Orgasm, she'll cry:

'Oh Paul, oh Paul ... oh Paul*!'

NB * Substitute bloke's name with the name of the bloke you're telling the joke to.

6

GREAT MYSTERIES OF OUR TIME (II) ... HOW COME?

How do **blokes** sort their **laundry**?

'Filthy' and 'filthy, but wearable'.

How does a bloke keep his youth?

By giving her money, diamonds and designer clothes.

How many **blokes** does it take to **change** a **light bulb**?

Two – one to change the bulb and one to collect the medal.

How do you stop a bloke biting his nails?

Make him wear shoes.

How many blokes does it take to put the toilet seat down?

Nobody knows. It hasn't happened yet.

How do you **stop** a **bloke** breaking into your **house**?

Replace all the locks with bra fasteners.

How do you get a bloke to climb up on the roof?

You tell him the drinks are on the house.

How do you **confuse** a **bloke**?

You don't, they're just born that way.

How many blokes does it take to change a light bulb?

Three – one to screw in the bulb, and two to listen to him brag about the screwing part.

How do you **start** a **conversation** with a **bloke** in a **flower shop**?

'So, what did you do?'

How do you stop blokes from spitting?

Turn down the grill.

How do you reply to a bloke who says: 'I knew that! I'm not a complete idiot, you know!'
'Oh! What part is missing then?'

How do you **kill** a **bloke**?
Ask him to jump off his ego and land on his IQ.

How many blokes does it take to change a light bulb?
As many as you like – it'll still be there waiting to be changed in the morning.

How do you stop your **bloke** reading your **email**?
Rename the mail folder 'instruction manuals'.

How do you spot the most popular bloke at the nudist colony?
He's the one who can have a cup of coffee in each hand and still carry a dozen doughnuts.

How do you know when a bloke's had an orgasm?
He snores.

How do you **make** a **bloke** scream when you are having **sex**?

Phone him.

How many men does it take to change a light bulb?

None, they just sit there in the dark and complain.

How do we know **blokes** invented **maps**?

Who else would turn an inch into a mile?

How can you spot a blind bloke at a nudist colony?

It isn't hard.

How many **men** does it take to **change** a **light bulb**?

None. They're happy living in the shadows.

How many bloke jokes are there?

None, they're all true.

7

DOCTOR, DOCTOR ...

A bloke goes to the doctor's and complains that he can't do all the things around the house that he used to do. When the examination is complete, the bloke says: 'C'mon, Doc, I can take it. Tell me in plain English what's wrong with me.'

'Well, in plain English,' replies the doctor, 'you're just lazy.'

'OK,' says the bloke. 'Now give me the medical term for it so I can tell my wife.'

A bloke hasn't been feeling well so he goes for a complete check-up. Afterwards the doctor comes out with the results …

'I'm afraid I have some very bad news,' says the doctor. 'You're dying, and you don't have much time left.'

'That's terrible,' says the bloke. 'How long have I got?'

'Ten,' the doctor says, sadly.

'Ten?' the bloke asks. 'Ten what? Months? Weeks? What?'

'Nine … Eight …'

A bloke goes to the doctor's and says: 'Doctor, I have an embarrassing sexual problem. I can't get it up for my wife any more.'

'Bring her in tomorrow,' says the doctor. 'Then I'll see what I can do.'

The following day the bloke returns with his wife. The doctor asks her to remove her clothes, turn all the way round, then lie down on the examining table. After asking her to get dressed again, he takes the bloke to one side and says: 'It's OK, you're in perfect health. Your wife doesn't give me an erection either!'

A bloke goes to see a psychiatrist wearing only clingfilm for shorts. The shrink says: **'Well, I can clearly see you're nuts.'**

A bloke goes to the doctor's because he's having problems getting an erection. After a complete examination the doctor tells him that the muscles around the base of his penis were damaged from a prior viral infection and the only option is an experimental treatment, if he were willing to take the risk. The treatment consists of implanting muscle tissue from an elephant's trunk in the bloke's penis.

The bloke thinks about it for a while. The idea of going through life without ever experiencing sex again is too much for him to bear. So, with the assurance that there would be no cruelty to the elephant, the bloke decides to go for it.

A few weeks after the operation, he's given the green light to use his newly renovated equipment so he plans a romantic evening with his girlfriend in one of the nicest restaurants in town.

However, half way through dinner he feels a stirring between his legs that continues to the point of being extremely painful. To release the pressure, he unzips his flies – and immediately his penis springs from his pants, goes to the top of the table, grabs a roll, then returns to his pants.

His girlfriend is stunned at first, but then with a sly smile on her face, says: 'That was incredible. Can you do it again?'

With his eyes watering, the bloke replies:

'I think I can, but I'm not sure if I can fit another roll up my arse.'

A family gather in a hospital waiting room where their relative lies gravely ill. Finally, the doctor comes in looking tired and sombre. 'I'm afraid I'm the bearer of bad news,' he says as he surveys the worried faces. 'The only hope left for your loved one at this time is a brain transplant. It's an experimental procedure, semi-risky and you'll have to pay for the brain yourselves.' The family members sit silent as they absorb the news. After a great length of time, someone asks: 'Well, how much does a brain cost?' The doctor quickly responds: '£5,000 for a bloke's brain, and £200 for a woman's brain.' The moment turns awkward. The men in the room try not to smile, avoiding eye contact with the women, but some actually smirk. One bloke, unable to control his curiosity, blurts out the question everyone wants to ask: 'Why is the bloke's brain so much more expensive?' The doctor smiles at his childish innocence and says: 'It's just standard pricing procedure. We have to mark down the price of the women's brains because they've actually been used.'

A bloke goes to the doctor's with a flywheel between his legs. The doctor asks: 'What's that?' And the bloke replies: 'I don't know, but it's driving me nuts!'

An 80-year-old bloke is having his annual check-up, and when the doctor asks him how he's feeling, he replies: 'I've never been better! I've got an 18-year-old bride who's pregnant with my child! What do you think about that?'

The doctor considers this for a moment, then says: 'Well, let me tell you a story. I know a bloke who's an avid hunter. He never misses a season. But one day he's in a bit of a hurry and he accidentally grabs his umbrella instead of his gun. So he's walking in the woods near a creek and suddenly spots a beaver in some brush in front of him! He raises up his umbrella, points it at the beaver and squeezes the handle. BAM!!! The beaver drops dead in front of him.'

'That's impossible!' says the old bloke in disbelief. 'Someone else must have shot that beaver.'

'My point, exactly.'

A bloke goes to see the doctor after a sudden illness. He takes his wife with him and after a thorough examination the doctor asks if he could speak to the wife for a moment. The bloke leaves the room while the doctor tells the wife the bad news. 'Your husband has a rare condition – any form of stress could instantly kill him so you must cater to his every whim. Make him breakfast, lunch and dinner. Make love to him whenever he requires. Don't give him any bad news at all. Is that understood?' The wife nods and then leaves to join her husband. Once outside, the bloke asks his wife: 'What did the doctor say?' She replies solemnly:

'He said you're going to die very soon.'

One day Paul complained to his mate, Simon: 'Blimey, my elbow really hurts. Do you think I should go and see a doctor?'

'No,' says Simon. 'There's a computer at the chemist's down the road that can diagnose anything far quicker than a doctor, just by analysing your urine. And it only costs a fiver.'

Paul figures he has nothing to lose so he wees into a jar and takes it to the chemist's. After he's put the sample and a fiver into the machine, it grinds into action and then spits out a small slip of paper, which reads: 'You have tennis elbow. Soak your arm in warm water. Avoid heavy work. It'll be better in two weeks.'

That evening, while thinking about how amazing this new technology is, Paul began to wonder whether the computer could be fooled. He decided to give it a try. He mixed up some tap water, a stool sample from his dog, urine samples from his wife and daughter, and to top it off, he masturbated into the concoction. He went back to the chemist's and, giggling, put the sample and a fiver into the computer. It made the usual noises, then spat out a slip of paper, which read: 'Your tap water is too hard – get a water softener. Your dog has ringworm – bathe him in anti-fungal shampoo. Your daughter is using cocaine – put her in a rehab clinic. Your wife is pregnant with twin girls. They're not yours – get a lawyer. And if you don't stop wanking, your tennis elbow will never get better!'

A bloke goes to the doctor's because he's been sunbathing too long and has got badly burnt.

'Yes,' says the doctor, after examining the bloke's whole body. 'It's definitely severe sunburn. I'll write you a prescription.'

Checking to see what the doctor had prescribed, the bloke was surprised that he'd written down calamine lotion and Viagra.

'That's odd,' says the bloke. 'I can see the need for the calamine lotion, but why the Viagra?'

And the doctor replies:

'That's to keep the sheets off you at night.'

A middle-aged bloke has a heart attack and while on the operating table he has a near-death experience. He sees God and asks if this is it. God says: 'No. You've got another 30 to 40 years left to live.'

When the bloke recovers he decides to stay in the hospital and have a face-lift, tummy tuck and hair implants, figuring that if he's got that long he may as well make the most of it.

Then, when he walks out of the hospital after the last operation he immediately gets hit by an ambulance. Arriving before God again, he says: 'I thought you said I'd got another 30 to 40 years.' To which God replies:

'To tell you the truth, I didn't recognise you!'

8

WHAT ARE THEY LIKE?!

Why are blokes like old bras?
They hang around your boobs all day and
give you no support when it's needed.

Why are blokes like photo-copiers?

You need them for reproduction, but that's about it.

Why are **blokes** like **textbooks**?

You have to spend a lot of time between the covers to gain a small amount of satisfaction.

Why are blokes like crystal?

Some look really good, but you can still see right through them.

Why are **blokes** like **lawnmowers**?

They're hard to get started, they emit noxious odours and half the time they don't work.

Why are blokes like fine wine?

They all start out like grapes, and it's our job to stomp
on them and keep them in the dark until they mature
into something you'd like to have dinner with.

Why are **blokes** like **newborn** babies?

They're cute at first, but pretty soon you get
tired of cleaning up their crap.

Why are blokes like curling tongs?

They're always hot and in your hair.

Why are **blokes** like **adverts**?

You can't believe a word they say.

Why are blokes like miniskirts?

If you're not careful, they'll creep up your legs.

Why are blokes like microwave meals?

They're both finished in 30 seconds.

Why are **blokes** like **bananas**?
The older they get, the less firm they are.

Why are **sensitive blokes** like **UFOs**?
You often hear about them, but you never see one.

Why are **blokes** like the **weather**?
You can't do anything to change either of them.

Why are **blokes** like **government bonds**?
Because they take so long to mature.

Why are **blokes** like **tights**?
They either cling, run or don't fit right in the crotch!

Why are **blokes** like **dogs**?

They're smelly, constantly demand food
and are both afraid of vacuum cleaners.

9

SO THIS BLOKE GOES INTO A PUB ...

A bloke's in the pub and decides he'd better go home, hoping he can manage to get back early enough so as not to piss his wife off for drinking after work. When he gets home, though, he finds her in bed with his boss. Later, back in the pub, he tells the barman what's just happened. 'That's awful,' says the barman. 'What did you do?'

'Well, I carefully sneaked back out the door and came back here. I mean, they were only just starting so I figured I had time for a couple more pints!'

Two blokes go on holiday together, and while Sam always has great success with the ladies, Ken gets nowhere.

'How can I impress the women like you do?' asks Ken. Sam gives him a potato, telling him that if he puts it in his trunks he can't fail. But after an hour of parading up and down the beach Ken gets disillusioned because he still hasn't pulled. 'It's no good, the potato trick hasn't worked,' says Ken in a sulk. Sam can barely contain his laughter when he spots the problem: 'No, you were meant to put it down the FRONT of your trunks!'

Two aliens are circling Earth, discussing its inhabitants. 'So what do you think? Intelligent life or not?' asks the first alien.

And the second answers: 'Hmm, the ones with the brains seem to be OK, but I'm not so sure about the ones with the balls!'

Gary asks John to help him mend his car after work, so they go back to Gary's place to get going in the garage. But before they start, Gary goes up to his wife, kisses her, tells her she's beautiful and how much he's missed her while he was out at work. When suppertime comes he compliments her on the meal she's cooked and tells her he loves her. Back in the garage later, John mentions his surprise at how attentive Gary is to his wife. Gary says that he started behaving like this a few months before and that it had really perked up their marriage.

John thinks it's got to be worth a try so when he gets home he gives his wife a massive hug, kisses her and tells her he loves her, but she just bursts into tears. John's confused and asks her why she's crying. 'This is the worst day of my life,' she says. 'First, little Jack fell off his bike and twisted his ankle, then the washing machine broke and flooded the kitchen. And now you come home drunk!'

A blond bloke, wanting to earn some money, decides to hire himself out as a handyman-type and starts canvassing a wealthy neighbourhood. He goes to the front door of the first house and asks the owner if she has any odd jobs. 'Well, how much would you charge to paint my porch?' she asks.

The blond bloke replies: 'How about £50?' and she agrees, telling him that the paint and other materials he might need are in the garage.

The woman's husband, inside the house, hears the conversation and says to his wife: 'Does he realise the porch goes all the way around the house?' To which she replies: 'He should, he was standing on it.'

A short time later, the blond bloke comes to the door to collect his money. 'You're finished already?' she asks. 'Yes,' he answers. 'And I had paint left over, so I gave it two coats.' Impressed, the woman reaches in her purse for the £50.

'And by the way,' the blond bloke adds.

'It's not a Porsche, it's a Ferrari!'

A fat bloke sees a notice in a shop window: 'A bed, a woman and a pie for £5.'

He goes into the shop and says to the owner: 'Is that right – a bed, a woman and a pie for only £5?'

'Of course,' says the shopkeeper.

'Sounds like a bargain, but what kind of pies are they?' asks the fat bloke.

This bloke walks into a bar and says: 'OUCH! Who put that there?'

This bloke goes to the Cup Final and notices that there's an empty seat between him and the next spectator. 'Imagine that,' he comments. 'Someone had a ticket for the most important game of the year and didn't turn up.' The guy next to him explains that the seat was for his wife, that every year they went to the final together, but she had died now and this was the first time he'd come on his own. 'That's awful!' says the first guy. 'Couldn't you have got a friend or relative to come with you?'

**'No,' he replies.
'Everyone I know is at her funeral.'**

A bloke goes before a judge to try to get excused from jury service, and the judge asks him why he can't serve as a juror. 'I don't want to be away from my job for that long,' replies the bloke.

'Can't they do without you at work?' asks the judge.

**'Yes,' says the bloke.
'But I don't want them to know it.'**

A bloke goes to Las Vegas on a gambling holiday that goes really badly for him. He loses everything except a dollar and the return air ticket, but knows if he can just get to the airport, he can get home. Outside the casino is a cab, so the bloke explains his situation to the cabbie. He promises to send the money from home, gives his address, his passport number, everything, but the cabbie just answers: 'If you don't have the $15 fare, get out of my cab!' so the poor bloke has to hitch-hike to the airport and only just catches his flight in time.

A year later, having worked really hard to build up his finances again, the bloke goes back to Vegas, figuring that this time he has to win. And he does – big time! When he leaves the casino to go back to the airport, he sees the miserable cabbie at the end of a long line of taxis and plans his revenge.

He gets into the first taxi in the queue and asks how much to go to the airport. 'Fifteen dollars,' comes the reply. 'And how much for you to give me a blow job on the way?' he asks. 'Get out of my cab!' screams the cabbie.

The bloke gets into the back of every taxi in the long queue and asks the same question, getting exactly the same reply from every cabbie. But when he gets to the cab of his old enemy, he just asks: 'How much to the airport?' Then, when the old cabbie says, 'Fifteen dollars,' he says, 'OK.'

Then, as they drive past the long line of cabs, the bloke gives a big smile and a thumbs-up to the rest of the cabbies.

A bloke gets a job working on a round-the-world cruise liner. At every port he sends his granny a beach photograph of himself, but one of the destinations was a nudist beach. He decides to have his picture taken anyway and cuts it in half. Two days later he's horrified when he realises he's sent his gran the wrong half of the photo, so he gets on the phone to try and explain what's happened.

'Gran, did you get my last photograph?' he asks.

'Yes, dear,' she says.

'But I think you should change your hairstyle – this one makes your nose look really big.'

Drugs Alert – Please Be Aware. Bloke Date Rape Drug

Police warn all blokes who are regular clubbers, party-goers and unsuspecting public-house regulars to be more alert and cautious when getting a drink offer from a girl. There is a drug called beer, which is essentially in liquid form. The drug is now being used by female sexual predators at parties to convince their male victims to have sex with them. The shocking statistic is that beer is available virtually anywhere!

All girls have to do is buy a beer or two for almost any bloke and simply ask him home for no-strings-attached sex. Blokes are literally rendered helpless against such attacks, which generally come from otherwise unattractive women who render their prey legless in order have their evil way. Please! Warn every bloke you know …

However, if you fall victim to this deceptive drug and the crooked women who are handing them out, there are male support groups with venues in every area, where you can discuss the details of your shocking encounter in an open and frank manner with a bunch of similarly affected, like-minded blokes.

For your nearest venue, simply look up 'Pub' in the *Yellow Pages*.

One night a woman finds her husband standing over their newborn baby's crib. Silently she watches him as the bloke's expression reveals disbelief, delight, amazement, scepticism and enchantment. Touched by this unusual display of deep emotion, she slips her arms round her husband. 'A penny for your thoughts,' she asks.

'It's amazing,' the bloke replies. 'I just can't see how anyone can make a cot like that for only £46.50.'

A bloke's in a quandary because he has to get rid of one of his staff. He's narrowed it down to one of two people, Debra or Jack, but it's a hard decision as they're both equally qualified and both do excellent work.

He finally decides that in the morning whichever one uses the water cooler first will have to go.

Debra comes in the next morning, hugely hung-over after partying all night. As she goes to the cooler to get some water to take an aspirin, the bloke approaches her and says: 'Debra, I've never done this before, but I have to lay you or Jack off.'

err....

Debra replies:

'Could you jack off, I've got a terrible headache.'

A woman goes to buy her boyfriend a pet for his birthday, but finds most of the ones in the shop too expensive, so she asks the shop assistant for advice.

'Well,' he said. 'I've got a large bullfrog going cheap, and they say it's been trained to give blow jobs. I can't prove it, but we have been selling a lot of them.'

The woman figures this would be a great joke gift anyway. And if it did give blow jobs, she'd never have to face them herself again.

When she gives her bloke the frog, she tells him about its supposed special skill and while he doesn't fall for it either, they have a good giggle about it and go to bed. In the middle of the night, though, she's woken up by the noise of pots and pans flying about downstairs in the kitchen. As she goes to investigate, she finds her bloke and the frog reading cookbooks.

'What are you two doing at this hour?' she asks. And the bloke replies:

'If I can teach this frog to cook, you're outta here!'

10

GREAT MYSTERIES OF OUR TIME (III) … WHAT'S ALL THAT ABOUT?

What's a bloke's idea of honesty in a relationship?
Telling you his real name.

What's a **bloke's** idea of **foreplay**?
Watching the end of the match first.

What do blokes use for birth control?

Their personalities.

What do you call that insensitive bit at the base of the penis?

A bloke.

What's the **fastest** way to a **bloke's** heart?

Through his chest with a sharp implement.

What do you call a bloke who says he's in touch with his feminine side?

A liar!

What should you give a bloke who has everything?

A woman to show him how to work it.

What's the best way to kill a bloke?

**Put a naked woman and a six-pack in front of him.
Then tell him to pick just one.**

What do you say to a bloke if he asks
you whether you fancy a quickie?
'As opposed to what?'

What do you call a **bloke**
with a **small willy**?
Justin . . .

What do single blokes have if mums have Mother's Day
and dads have Father's Day?
Palm Sunday.

What's the **definition**
of **mixed emotions**?
Watching the bloke who just dumped
you crash into your spanking new car.

What should you do with your bum before having sex?
Drop him off at the golf club.

What happens when a vain and irritating bloke takes Viagra?

He gets taller.

What do you call a **man** who does the **washing up**, cleaning and is always **polite** and **helpful**?

A wo-man.

What do you call a **bloke** with a **big willy** and **lots of cash**?

Darling.

What is six-inches long, three-inches wide
and drives women wild?

A £50 note!

What do you call a **bloke** with an **IQ** of **five**?

Gifted.

What does it mean when a bloke is in your bed, gasping
for breath and calling your name?

You didn't hold the pillow down long enough.

What do you call a **woman** with half a **brain cell**?

A bloke.

What do you call a **zit** on a **bloke's penis**?

A brain tumour.

What do you call a fly in a bloke's brain?

Space invader.

What should you say to a bloke whose chat-up line is: 'Do you want to come home and sit on my face?'

'Why, is your nose bigger than your penis?'

What should you do if you see your ex-boyfriend rolling around in pain on the ground?

Shoot him again.

What did the elephant say to the naked bloke?

How do you drink with that?

What's more useful –
a **bloke** or a **chocolate fireguard**?

Well, a chocolate fireguard can make a lovely sauce.

What's got eight arms and an IQ of 60?

**Four blokes watching
a football game.**

What do you call a **bunch of blokes** in a **circle**?

A dope ring.

What's the definition of a male chauvinist pig?

A bloke who hates every bone in a woman's body, except his own.

What's a **bloke's** idea of **romance**?

You go and fetch him another can after sex.

What makes blokes **chase women** they have **no** intention of **marrying**?
The same urge that makes dogs chase cars they have no intention of driving.

What's the definition of a bloke?

A vibrator with a wallet!

What did the **elephant** say to the **bloke**?
'It's cute, but can you pick up peanuts with it?!'

What's the best form of birth control for a bloke over 50?

Nudity.

11

WOMEN ON TOP

A bloke's at his wedding rehearsal and decides he wants to start married life with the upper hand. He takes the vicar aside and says: 'Look, I'll give you £100 if you'll change the wedding vows. Can you leave in the "love, honour and obey" bit and take out "forsaking all others, be faithful only unto her"?' The bloke then passes the vicar the cash and walks away smugly.

The day of the wedding arrives and when it comes to the groom's vows, the vicar looks him straight in the eye and says: 'Will you promise to prostrate yourself before her, obey her every command and wish, serve her breakfast in bed every morning of your life and swear eternally before God and your lovely wife that you will never even look at another women, as long as you both shall live?'

The groom gulps and looks around, then says in a tiny voice: 'I will.'

After the service the furious groom takes the vicar aside again and hisses: 'I thought we had a deal!'

The vicar gives him back his £100 and whispers back: 'She made me a much better offer.'

A bloke steps on to one of those speak-your-weight machines that also tell your fortune.

'Listen to this,' he tells his wife, showing her a small white card. 'It says I'm energetic, bright, resourceful and a great lover.'

'Yes,' his wife nods. **'And it's got your weight wrong, too!'**

Two women are sitting on a park bench, when along comes a bloke.

Women: 'We bet you that we can guess your age!'

Bloke: 'Go on then! Bet you can't.'

Women: 'OK – we need you to take your trousers down!'

Bloke: 'Errrrr, OK.'

Women: 'And now we need you to take your pants down!'

Bloke: 'What? Er, OK then.'

Women: 'You're 27!'

Bloke: 'WOW! Amazing! I am 27 – you could tell that just by looking at my bits?'

Women: 'No, you told us yesterday.'

A boring bloke says to his wife: 'Honey, why are you wearing your wedding ring on the wrong finger?'

And the bored wife replies: 'Because I married the wrong man!'

Ten blokes and one woman are hanging on to a rope beneath a helicopter. They know there are too many on the rope and that if someone doesn't get off, the rope will break and they'll all die, but they can't decide who should make the sacrifice. Finally, the woman gives a really touching speech, saying how she'll give up her life to save the others because women are used to giving up things for their husbands and children, offering themselves to blokes and not receiving anything in return. When she finishes speaking, all the blokes applaud her bravery.

Proving that blokes should never underestimate the intelligence of a woman.

A woman finds an old lamp in the attic and when she polishes it, a genie pops out and offers to grant her three wishes. However, he warns her that whatever she wishes for, the bloke in her life will get ten times better or more. So the woman thinks about this and says: 'For my first wish, I'd like to be the most beautiful woman in the world.' The genie says: 'OK, but remember your bloke will be the most handsome man in the world and every woman will lust after him.' The woman replies: 'Go ahead.' So sure enough, she's the world's most beautiful woman. 'For my second wish, I want to be the richest woman in the world.' The genie warns: 'That will make your bloke ten times richer than you.' 'Fine by me,' is the reply. So she's the richest woman in the world. The genie asks: 'What is your final wish?' Her reply: 'I'd like a very mild heart attack!'

A bloke is sitting quietly reading his paper one morning when his wife sneaks up behind him and whacks him on the back of his head with a huge frying pan.

Bloke: 'What was that for?'

Wife: 'What was that piece of paper in your jacket pocket with the name "Marianne" written on it?'

Bloke: 'Remember two weeks ago when I went to the races? "Marianne" was the name of one of the horses I bet on.'

The wife looks sheepish, apologises and goes to put the frying pan back in the kitchen.

Three days later he's once again sitting in his chair reading and she repeats the frying-pan attack.

Bloke: 'What the hell was that for this time?'

Wife: 'Your horse phoned.'

Three blokes are out fishing, when out of the blue they catch a mermaid. She begs to be set free and offers to grant each of them a wish to let her go. One of the blokes doesn't believe it, and says: 'OK, if you can really grant wishes, double my IQ.' The mermaid says: 'Done.' Suddenly, the bloke starts reciting Shakespeare flawlessly and analysing it with extreme insight.

The second bloke is so amazed, he says to the mermaid: 'Triple my IQ.' The mermaid says: 'Done.' And the bloke starts to spout out the mathematical solutions to problems that have been stumping the world's greatest mathematicians.

The last bloke is so enthralled with the changes in his friends that he says to the mermaid: 'Quintuple my IQ.' The mermaid looks at him and says: 'I normally don't try to change people's minds when they make a wish, but I really wish you'd reconsider.'

The bloke says: 'No, I want you to increase my IQ times five, and if you don't do it, I won't set you free.'

'Please,' says the mermaid. 'You don't know what you're asking ... it'll change your entire view on the universe. Ask for something else ... a million dollars, anything?' But no matter what the mermaid said, the bloke insisted on having his IQ increased by five times its usual power.

So the mermaid sighs and says: 'Done.'

And he becomes a woman ...

A bloke walks into the bedroom to find his wife jumping up and down on the bed. She says: 'I've just had my annual check-up and the doctor says I may be 45, but I've got the breasts of an 18 year old!'

'Yeah,' says the bloke. 'And what did he say about your 45-year-old arse?'

'Oh, he didn't mention you, dear.'

An **obnoxious bloke** tries to **apologise** to a **female** colleague, saying: 'I'm **sorry** I put you in such an **awkward position** the other day.' Not feeling in a **forgiving mood,** she replies:

'There's not a position between one and 69 that I'd ever care to be in with you.'

A bloke and a woman are involved in a terrible car accident. Both of their cars are totally demolished, but amazingly, neither of them is hurt. After they crawl out of their cars, the woman says: 'So, you're a man? That's interesting. I'm a woman. Wow, just look at our cars! There's nothing left, but fortunately, we're unhurt. This must be a sign from God that we should meet and be friends, and live together in peace for the rest of our days.' Flattered, the man replied: 'Oh yes, I agree with you completely! This must be a sign from God!'

The woman continued: 'And look at this, here's another miracle: my car is completely demolished but this bottle of wine didn't break. Surely God wants us to drink this wine and celebrate our good fortune.' Then she hands the bottle to the man. The man nods his head in agreement, opens the bottle and drinks half of it and then hands it back to the woman. The woman takes the bottle, immediately puts the cap back on and hands it back to the man. The man asks: 'Aren't you having any?' The woman replies: 'No, I think I'll wait for the police.'

A newly-wed couple are just beginning their honeymoon. The bloke takes off his trousers, gives them to the girl and tells her to put them on. They're four sizes too big, so she says: 'There's no way I can wear these.'

'Good,' he replies. 'Now you know who wears the trousers in this relationship.'

Then she takes her tiny knickers off and says: 'OK, put these on.'

'I can't get into them,' the bloke says.

And she replies: 'Correct, unless you change your attitude.'

If you have an intelligent woman, an intelligent bloke and Santa Claus in a lift, which one is the odd one out?

The intelligent woman – because the other two DON'T EXIST.